# PENGUIN WORLD

# PENGUIN WORLD

## Ian J. Strange

Illustrated with photographs and
with drawings by the author

DODD, MEAD & COMPANY, NEW YORK

Library of Congress Cataloging in Publication Data

Strange, Ian J.
Penguin world.

Includes index.
Summary: Discusses the characteristics and behavior
of the many species of penguins, particularly those that
annually return to the Falkland Islands off the coast
of Argentina.
1. Penguins—Juvenile literature.   2. Birds—Falkland
Islands—Juvenile literature.   [1. Penguins.   2. Birds—
Falkland Islands]   I. Title.
QL696.S47S87       598.4′41       81-43228
ISBN 0-396-08000-6                 AACR2

PICTURE CREDITS:

Wolfgang Kähler, 19, 20-21 and Peter Richards, 114-115.
All other photographs and drawings are by Ian J. Strange.

To many good friends, some anonymous, who share
that interest in the conservation of such creatures

# Contents

# Introduction

Just over half a mile from the house where most of our studies are recorded, within sound and smell, is a vast colony of rockhopper penguins mixed with other seabirds. Farther away we can see colonies of gentoo and Magellan penguins. This is New Island, a small remote island within the Falkland Islands group, which my wife and I operate as a wildlife reserve.

For some years we have watched and recorded the lives of the various species of penguins here. Now we would like to convey something of the wonders of the world of these penguins through one of our favorite subjects, the rockhopper penguin.

There are some eighteen different species of penguins found in different parts of the Southern Hemisphere. In this story of the

*High up on the New Island cliff tops thousands of rockhopper penguins form their colonies, along with king cormorants and black-browed albatrosses.*

rockhoppers, which is typical of this family of birds, we have brought in details of the other four species which are found in the Falkland Islands, and we have mentioned species from other areas. Space within the covers of this book, however, does not allow us to do more than briefly mention these other equally fascinating species.

# 1

# What Is a Penguin?

Penguins are flightless birds that have become adapted to a life spent largely at sea. Their wings have been modified to become very sturdy, short flippers, which enable them to dive and swim great distances. Their short overall feathering keeps them dry and warm. The tips of their feathers are oily, thus repelling water. Their coats are shed each year and replaced by new plumage. Their bodies are equipped with thick layers of fat, or blubber, where food and water are stored. This fat also provides them with additional insulation to permit prolonged swimming in waters colder than their own body temperatures.

On land, penguins walk in an upright position. Their short thickset legs and feet allow many species only to waddle or hop. Whichever their manner of walking, penguins look rather ungainly but endearing as they make their awkward way along. Once in the water, however, they are master swimmers and show extreme speed and efficiency. Their hard flippers, covered with

scaly feathers, are used to propel them through the water, their stiff tails acting as rudders. When they swim fast, they porpoise out of the water at intervals to breathe. Otherwise they can float on the surface with their heads out of the water, tails sometimes protruding stiffly.

Although their plumage, generally speaking, appears black and white, some penguins have bright and colorful patches on the sides of their heads. Some have brilliant crests. Eyes, facial patterns, and bills vary according to species. Penguins also differ in size. The largest—the emperor—is over three feet tall, and the smallest— the little blue—measures only some fifteen inches. Their height

Penguins are flightless
birds with short flippers,
which enable them to dive
and swim. On land,
penguins walk in an
upright position.

Below: Penguin species
differ considerably in size.
Note how much smaller
the rockhopper in the
foreground is compared
to the gentoo.

can alter when they stretch their necks or push themselves up on their toes. They have webbed feet like most other seabirds. Male and female birds are alike, but males are generally larger and have heavier bills than the females.

Each species of penguin has a distinctive voice or call which serves to identify others of its kind at sea. The voices of different species of penguins differ from shrill notes to long drawn-out braying sounds, raucous calls, and trumpeting. Some of these calls are peacefully haunting when heard on a quiet summer's evening, others can be grating and rusty to the human ear. Each plays an important part in the life cycles of the penguins.

## Where Penguins Are Found

Penguins spend much of their lives at sea, coming ashore to breed and rear their young. Although generally associated with icy polar regions, not all penguins breed in cold zones. There are eighteen known species of penguins, and all of them breed in the Southern Hemisphere. One species, however, is found close to the equator.

Certain parts of Australia, New Zealand, South Africa, and South America, and particularly many smaller groups of islands in the Antarctic and sub-Antarctic zones hold vast populations of penguins. In the slightly warmer or sub-Antarctic zones, besides numbers, there is also a greater variety of penguins. Some of the colonies number millions of birds. The northernmost breeding places for penguins are as far up the Pacific Ocean as Peru and the Galápagos Islands, quite near the equator.

*Gentoos and rockhoppers coming ashore to a remote breeding island in the Falklands.*

Most of the sites chosen by penguins to establish their breeding colonies are remote. These colonies are located close to ample supplies of food, for which the birds forage daily when rearing their young. Only three species of penguins nest in icy and snowy conditions of south polar regions, and a similar number of species breed in subtropical areas, such as the Cape Province of South Africa.

Generally penguins are *colonial* breeders and much prefer living in groups than alone. Those birds which do not gather together in large nesting groups have secluded and safe underground burrows (like the Magellan penguin in the Falkland Islands), or they may breed under bushes or among lush vegetation. One species—the emperor penguin—found in Antarctica, forms large colonies on sea ice to breed and bring up its chicks, and fishes for food among the ice floes.

On some islands more than one species may share the same breeding grounds, but usually penguins nest in groups of their own kind even within another's neighborhood. At sea, they seem to keep together as well, and it is believed each species has its own feeding zones.

## KINDS OF PENGUINS

All penguins belong to the family Spheniscidae. Penguins, like all living things, are classified for scientific purposes into groups or species. In very simple terms, these can be summarized as follows:

The emperor and king, or wingless divers (*Aptenodytids*), are the largest and most colorful of the penguins. They have bright golden patches on their throats and upper necks. Emperors have their colonies on the sea ice in Antarctica. This is the most southerly breeding ground for any species of bird. Their breeding cycle is also unique. They lay their eggs in May-June (southern winter), incubate during the coldest period and when it is dark for much

*Portrait of an adult king penguin.*

16

of the day as well as night. It is the male bird that incubates the single egg, with birds huddling together to keep warm. During this time the female stays at sea, to return when the young chick is about to hatch. During the late winter and early spring the chick is reared by the parents, so that it is ready to go to sea on its own in January. At this time the sea ice is broken up and there is a plentiful supply of food.

The king penguins, slightly smaller than emperors, live on low-latitude Antarctic and sub-Antarctic islands. Some of their breeding places are on South Georgia, Macquarie Island, Prince Edward Island, and the Crozet Islands, and a small colony has become established in the Falkland Islands. This is the most northerly place of their range. Their rather unusual breeding cycle will be discussed in more detail later.

Although probably not too widely known, the yellow-eyed penguin of New Zealand and some of its northern offshore islands has been studied carefully in that country. It stands under a genus of its own, *Megadyptes*, meaning large divers. Yellow-eyed penguins nest in coastal areas, cleverly concealed with tussock grass and thick scrub. Unlike many penguin species, the yellow-eyed remains close to its breeding grounds all the year round and does not migrate.

Three kinds of penguin fall under the group of *Pygoscelids* (brush-tailed). These are gentoo, chinstrap, and Adélie. Adélies

*Adélie penguins are found nesting in Antarctica.*

are predominantly black-and-white stocky birds with distinctive white eye-rings. They form large colonies on several localities on the Antarctic peninsula and also nest on the South Orkneys, South Shetlands, and other islands.

The chinstrap penguin's name does justice to its looks. It has white cheeks, a black crown, and a thin black line which extends from ear to ear across the white throat. Some colonies of chinstrap penguins are very dense and number many tens of thousands of

birds. These are mainly in the South American part of Antarctica, on islands of the Scotia Arc and others.

The gentoo penguin is a little more colorful than the other brush-tailed penguins, with an orange-red bill and feet a shade of orange-pink. It has white flecking forming a patch across the top of the head. Gentoos breed on South Georgia, South Sandwich, South Orkney, and South Shetland Islands, and also on Macquarie, Heard, Kerguélen, and other islands. They also live as far north as the Falkland Islands.

Then come the crested penguins forming the genus *Eudyptes*, meaning beautiful divers. There are several species of crested penguins. These are smaller penguins and each kind has a slightly different golden crest and other characteristics which enable identification.

Rockhopper penguins nest in colonies, generally among rocks and boulders, often on top of cliffs which other penguins would have difficulty reaching. They spend a long time each year at sea, returning regularly to their breeding sites. In the Falkland Islands some of their colonies are shared by a few pairs of macaroni penguins, and on Campbell Island by other crested penguins.

*A rockhopper penguin colony among the rocks and boulders.*

Rockhoppers range from Macquarie, Kerguélen, Marion, Prince Edward, and Crozet Islands in the south, to the Falkland Islands and possibly islands near Cape Horn. A subspecies nests on the Tristan da Cunha group of islands, Gough Island, Amsterdam, and others.

Macaroni penguins are heavier built and have more massive bills than the rockhoppers. They have orange-yellow eyebrow feathering which joins on the forehead. These birds nest in huge numbers on South Georgia and on the South Sandwich, South Orkney, and South Shetland Islands. Macquarie, Kerguélen, Heard, Prince Edward, Bouvet, and Marion Islands also hold populations of macaroni penguins. Recent population studies of those nesting at South Georgia have shown that some nine million birds are to be found there.

Other crested species are the erect-crested, royal, Snares Island, and Fjordland penguins.

The wedge-shaped penguins (*Spheniscids*) include the Magellan and Peruvian penguins, the black-footed or jackass, and Galápagos penguins.

These are all black-and-white birds with different facial markings and bands on faces, necks, and upper breasts. These birds are sometimes colonial, and in other instances solitary. Magellan pen-

*Adult macaroni penguin. This species is larger than the rockhopper, with a golden orange crest which joins in the center of the forehead.*

*An adult Magellan penguin.*

guins belong in southern South America and the Falkland Islands.

The Peruvian penguin lives on islands off the coasts of Peru and Chile, feeding in the cool Humboldt current waters. They, as well as the black-footed species in South Africa and the Galápagos penguins near the equator, nest in caverns or burrows and in cool shady shelter.

In Patagonia, South America, the Magellan—Magellanic—penguin nests on sandy or shingle coastal areas and on some islets offshore. In the Falkland Islands they burrow under peaty banks or beneath tussock-grass plants. Because of their braying call they are locally called jackass penguins, a confusion with the South African species (black-footed) which also bears this name.

The fairy or little blue penguins of southern Australia and New Zealand fall under the group of *Eudyptula,* meaning small beautiful divers. They are very small, colored blue, and have nocturnal habits. These birds come ashore in the evening and leave at dawn; only those birds courting, incubating, or molting are found ashore during the day. They nest in well-concealed spots, caves, or burrows.

As mentioned in the introduction, the story of the wonders of the world of penguins will be told through our studies of the rockhopper penguins which live in the Falkland Islands. These islands lie in the South Atlantic Ocean some three hundred miles northeast of Cape Horn (the southernmost tip of South America). This group of islands is rather unique since five species of penguins breed there. The rockhoppers are the most numerous.

# 2

# Return from the Sea

Each spring, which in the Southern Hemisphere means September/ October, thousands of rockhopper penguins (*Eudyptes crestatus*) return from their winter migration at sea to their age-old colonies, or *rookeries*. Another precise breeding cycle begins.

Rockhopper penguin rookeries in the Falkland Islands are generally located in exposed, rocky sites. The birds build nests close to one another, sometimes among boulders or protected by tussock grass. We are going to dwell here with the rockhoppers which populate one particular colony on New Island, one of the Falklands' most remote western isles. The colony—one of several— lies on the brow of a hill and extends for over twenty acres, densely covering ground which slopes from a tussock-covered area to sheer cliffs, which drop down to the sea three hundred feet below. As

*One of the New Island rockhopper penguin colonies, spreading into the thick tussock grass, which the penguins often use as nesting material.*

31

*Following a well-worn route, rockhoppers make their way from shore to colony. On these trails, the rocky surfaces become deeply grooved and polished by the passage of so many birds over many years.*

elsewhere in the Falklands, the colony is shared by several thousand black-browed albatrosses and king cormorants. A small number of macaroni penguins, a species quite uncommon in the Falklands, although numerous farther south, are known to breed in these same colonies. These other birds are fully accepted by the rockhoppers, which far outnumber all their neighbors.

The rockhoppers, as their name implies, can hop over ledges and stones. They have to climb steep narrow paths to their nest sites and do it easily. These routes are well worn and show the passage of thousands of birds. Their claw marks over centuries have carved grooves deep into the hard rocks, and their thick-soled feet have polished many rocks like marble.

During the first week in October, the colony is empty except for the handsome black-browed albatrosses, which return to their nests

*The black-browed albatrosses are close nesting companions on many of the rockhopper penguin colonies in the Falkland Islands.*

in September. During the second week in October the first penguin arrivals may be seen, standing in little groups, very still, as though resting from their exerting journey across the sea. Throughout the next few days, reaching a peak by the middle of the month, more and more birds are obvious in the rookeries, generally returning in small groups. This points to the possibility that birds from specific "neighborhoods" stay together at sea and return home at the same time.

On close inspection, we discover that the majority of these penguins are male birds. They have slightly heavier builds and have thicker bills than female rockhoppers. The males return earliest to the rookeries to prepare the nest sites in anticipation of the females' homecoming. We knew that the same nest sites were used by the same birds season after season, but it was nonetheless exciting and delightful to see birds that we had marked with flipper bands one year come back the next. They were busily collecting nest materials and marking out the sites that they had abandoned at the end of the previous season.

Concentrations of diligent penguins walk or hop around attending to business, their bills soiled from collecting blades of tussock grass, bits of rock, bones, and pebbles, and gradually furnishing the nests. The nests vary in appearance from quite simple scrapings with little lining to rather substantial structures.

*After arrival ashore, the rockhoppers stand and dry off their feathers before entering the colonies.*

*Male and female rockhopper penguins. The male is in the foreground and can be identified by its heavier bill.*

After another week, we notice the arrival of the first females. A great deal of activity can now be seen. As the number of birds pairing up increases, so does the volume of noise as the penguins display to each other in greeting and courtship. We know that the females return to their same mate each season, but we can only wonder about the possibility of the pair remaining at sea together. No doubt this will remain as one of nature's secrets for many years yet.

On meeting at the nest site, both birds throw back their flippers, perhaps in recognition, perhaps for balance. At the same time, their heads are raised as they make their greeting calls. Listening carefully, one notes that the calls are different. Also we see that the male bird generally raises his head higher than his mate's and shakes it from side to side. As the season progresses neighboring penguins will join in the greeting display, developing a *group bond* which will play an important role in the rookery later.

Once the females are home, they often take over the nests. The males, however, appear to remain solely responsible for the collection of nesting material, which continues to be added as part of

*The male rockhopper penguin collects and presents nest material to the female as part of courtship.*

the courtship activities. It is with care and tenderness that the male will be seen bringing a twig, or a stone—often taken from a nearby nest when its occupants are not looking!—and laying his offering by the female bird to add to their nest. He will be greeted noisily and ecstatic calls will take place, sometimes followed by mutual preening.

*Preening* is the basic and most important part of any bird's feather care. The bill is used to clean, arrange, and oil the feathers. On land and at sea a penguin spends a lot of time preening by stroking and nibbling at its feathers with the bill, which may first remove small amounts of oil from its oil gland (situated at the base of the tail). This oil then helps to waterproof its feathers. Mutual preening, where a pair preens each other, is commonly seen among the rockhoppers, especially when attention is being given to the feathers on the head.

But not all is love and care. Rockhopper penguins can be most aggressive against intruders. They defend their territories quite tenaciously. Adopting a low posture, neck and body outstretched and flippers almost horizontal with the ground, the rockhoppers will ward off offending trespassers, more often than not by pecking them fiercely.

Now that the nests are ready and pair bonds are established, mating follows. The first egg is laid eleven days later, at the beginning of November. The second egg, which completes the *clutch*, is laid four or five days after the first. Only at this point do the birds start to *incubate*, or sit on the eggs. Prior to the presence

*Rockhopper pairs defend their territories with vigor.*

of the second egg in the nest the brooding instinct does not seem to be developed, and the birds, in most cases, merely stand over the egg.

The eggs of the rockhopper penguin are a very delicate blue-white color when laid. The fairly smooth shell quickly turns white with a chalklike texture to the surface. The eggs are almost round

but with quite a pronounced point at the smaller end, and are about double the size of a hen's egg. There are small variations between the first and second eggs. Contrary to what has been believed generally to apply to all crested penguins, the smaller first egg is not discarded in the Falkland Islands species. Both are incubated by the parent birds.

For just over a month, thousands of pairs of rockhopper parents share incubation of the eggs. The colonies assume a very quiet and peaceful atmosphere. Silence is broken only by intermittent, but brief, display calls. The guard over the nest and eggs changes in a most natural fashion: one of a pair will suddenly leave the nest, and its partner will immediately and automatically take over, carefully tucking the egg beneath the *brood patch*. This is an area of the bird's belly that has lost the down feathers and which is richly supplied with blood vessels which allow the transfer of heat from parent to eggs. It becomes quite noticeable in breeding birds at this time, showing a small pink cavity in the otherwise white feathering. One bird sits on the eggs, the other "stands watch" close behind. There is no fuss over this change, which is repeated several times during the first two weeks of incubation.

In most cases, penguins sit very tightly over their nests. But the more inexperienced breeders may lose their eggs to some of the predators, such as the Falkland skua. This bird, which in some areas feeds almost exclusively from the rookeries, takes eggs or

*The male rockhopper takes over incubation while the female rests.*

young chicks. Dolphin gulls and others will also try to snatch some eggs here and there.

Up to this point—toward the end of November—daily observations showed a fairly consistent pattern of events in the colonies. Then suddenly, one morning, a most remarkable sight met our eyes: where were many of the birds? The tightly packed effect was not so obvious. There were spaces between birds. On closer study we discovered that in the majority of cases, breeding birds were no longer in pairs, but female rockhoppers alone incubated and guarded their clutches. Their mates had gone to sea to feed for the first time since their arrival in the colonies over a month ago. Within two or three days thousands of male birds had departed.

One of the reasons why penguins can remain on land for long periods, without going to sea where they feed, is because they are equipped with an underblanket of fat, known as subdermal fat. This provides them with storage for food and water. It helps also to insulate them from the weather and from those equally long periods they do spend at sea. Their roomy stomachs are able to hold substantial quantities of food, which is suitable and necessary for their feeding habits. In spite of this ability to "fast" for long periods, most of the birds showed signs of lack of food. Loss of weight had become quite obvious. The clean, fat, bright-crested and shiny-plumaged birds which were courting and displaying a few weeks ago now had become very thin.

But now the birds were renewing their energy with nourishment. Adverse weather and very heavy seas did not appear to

*The skua preys on penguin colonies, taking eggs or chicks.*

matter to them one bit. They made their way down to the shore
and plunged into the ocean regardless of the weather.

For approximately ten days hardly any male breeding birds were

*At one point, only the male rockhoppers remain in the colonies incubating while their partners feed.*

to be found in the colonies. How far they range on these foraging voyages we do not know.

The overall picture changes again with a noticeable return of spotless birds coming to relieve the sitting females. The exchange does not take place right away, and for a few days both birds are together once more, exchanging calls, preening each other, or adding material to their nests. Incubation change-overs are once more routine. Shortly afterward, it is the females that "desert" on a much-needed feeding trip.

The more aggressive males are responsible for guarding the eggs during the last stage of incubation. The male is present when, after thirty-three days, a hole, at first no bigger than a pinhead, starts to develop on the egg. Cheeping calls can be heard from within the egg and often the chick's tapping with its bill, making its way out into the world. The egg is about to hatch, but it will take twenty-four hours for the baby penguin actually to emerge from the shell. The guarding parent will frequently bow low over the hatching egg and call loudly, giving its young an identification call which will play an important role later on in its life.

Macaroni penguins in the rockhopper colony follow much the same pattern of nest building and breeding. But in a colony of gentoo penguins (*Pygoscelis papua*) things are a bit different. Gentoos are a resident species and their breeding grounds rarely are vacated completely. They also start building their nests the first week in October, and the first eggs are laid by the middle of

Macaroni penguin with egg. The nest has been built from wing bones of an albatross!

the month. But unlike the rockhoppers, gentoo penguins choose for their nesting grounds a variety of sites. They may nest on coastal grasslands where ample supplies of "diddle-dee," or red crowberry shrub, can be used as nesting material, or on flat rocky islands devoid of vegetation. Their nests may be scooped out of sand or mounded from stones, dried mud, or small pebbles. Over

*Gentoos nesting among "diddle-dee" (red crowberry) shrub, which they pull from the ground to form nests.*

*On arrival back at the colony, adult gentoos call and display.*

a period of years their colonies usually move inland in a gradual way due to the birds' quest for fresh nesting materials. They have been known to walk as far as three miles inland from a landing zone to their nests. It is not uncommon to see them, their white fronts gleaming in the light, a long line of waddling figures going across greens and traversing low hills on their routes home from the sea.

The Magellan penguins (*Spheniscus magellanicus*) use the same nests each season, and one wonders in awe how these creatures are able to locate their own burrows in areas where the ground seems to be peppered with hundreds of underground nests.

*Pair of adult Magellans, at home among tussock grass.*

But find them they do. Using their bills to pull and pry away the earth, and their feet to scrape out the loosened matter, the Magellan penguins often dig burrows well over a yard in length with a sizable "cavern" at the end, where a nest is built of grass and other vegetation. This species and other wedge-shaped penguins—Galápagos, Peruvian, and jackass or black-footed—together with the species of blue and fairy penguins, are the only penguins which nest underground or in situations which give them this feeling.

To illustrate how the Magellanic penguins find their own burrows we can relate how on one particularly extensive breeding ground in the Falklands, a solitary male Magellan penguin—for it is the male in this species that returns first also—was seen coming ashore one fine September day. He came up the wide sandy beach from the sea and, without any hesitation, made his way some three hundred yards inland, past dozens and dozens of burrows. At one point only did he stop to glance just for a moment about him and then, making a decisive right-angle turn, continued on a few yards and promptly went into a burrow, where he remained. That was the very first arrival. Within three or four days the coast was occupied by a myriad of its kind returning from migration. All the burrows would soon have occupants once more, peering at you in their particular way, straining their necks out and looking first out of one eye, then rolling their heads around to study you with their other eye.

The egg-laying dates of gentoo penguins coincide with those of the Magellans, whose return to the breeding burrows takes place with amazing regularity about mid-September each year. Incubation periods of gentoo and Magellan penguins in the Falklands vary little, both species taking just over a month. When rockhopper chicks come out of their shells, chick rearing at the other penguin colonies is already in full swing.

The most colorful of the Falkland penguins is the king, and this species differs not only in its looks but also in its breeding habits from other penguins described. We shall discuss this penguin separately.

A rockhopper penguin
chick shortly after
emerging from the egg.

Parents keep a close watch
over their offspring.

# 3

# A Home on Land

A few days after hatching, the rockhopper chick is no more than a little ball of gray fluff, but soon it grows and puts on weight. Carefully guarded by its parents during the first few weeks of its life, it lives tucked against the nesting adult, which sits virtually over its offspring offering warmth and protection. The young will soon be seen and heard begging for food—a pleading and constant piping call, while its little upturned head shakes from side to side.

Feeding is carried out by *regurgitation*, which means that the food taken at sea by a parent bird is only partially digested and held in the parent's stomach by a special "mechanism" in its body system. Upon the parent's return to the nest, it partially vomits food which the young chick takes from the adult's mouth. During the first few days of its life, the young penguin receives very small quantities of a mucuslike substance; as it grows, the amount and contents alter gradually.

This secretion of mucuslike substance, which is produced in the

*While the returning parent feeds the young chick, its mate stands close guard.*

stomachs of the adult birds, is believed by some scientists to be the "mechanism" which restricts digestion of the food. Watching the action of feeding, we wondered if there was also a simpler explanation for the formation of this substance. It is possible that it helped the passage of food from adult to chick, especially when the young bird has to be fed on very small samples of krill. We found that krill regurgitated by adults was generally rather dry. If it had not been for the covering of mucus holding quantities of krill together—rather like sausage meat within its skin—the process of regurgitation and passage to the chick would be much more difficult.

Once fed, it is not uncommon to see the chicks, visibly full and

*Plump and well fed, the chicks grow quickly.*

*A family of striated caracara (or "Johnny rooks") at their nest site, overlooking a colony of rockhoppers, on which they prey.*

exhausted, lying flat on their stomachs with their heads in the protected shelter of the parents' brood patches. Or they may sit facing away from the adult birds, their white downy bellies literally bulging.

Although a large percentage of rockhoppers lays and incubates two eggs, only a few pairs are able successfully to rear two young. In some cases, when an egg cracks and the first young of a clutch hatches, it is easy for the second egg to be misplaced in the nest, where the parent is not able to continue its incubation. In other instances, not helped by the rocky and sloping terrain, an egg may roll away from a nest site. The adult rockhopper does not make any attempt to retrieve an egg once it leaves the immediate vicinity of its nest. Similarly, when both eggs hatch successfully, one of the chicks may be lost in the early days, either through lack of sufficient food or because somehow it manages to stray too far from the parent's reach. Predators then come into action and will snatch an unguarded egg or young chick in a flash.

As their name implies, predators are birds and animals which prey on other species. In the particular case of the rockhopper penguins in the Falkland Islands, the main predators are skuas and a rare bird of prey, the striated caracara. The wattled sheath-

*Wattled sheathbill, a scavenger of penguin colonies. This bird breeds farther south but is a common visitor to rookeries in the Falkland Islands.*

bill is one of the scavengers feeding off the rookeries. These are some of the penguins' enemies on land, taking mainly eggs and young chicks. The skuas are particularly active in the colonies under study by us, swooping down to take unguarded eggs or young birds. On islands which hold large populations of striated caracara—locally known as "Johnny rooks"—these bold and immensely interesting birds are the only predators on penguin colonies. Gulls and vultures are also scavengers, taking what they can find lying about the colonies but not actually taking live prey, although the dolphin gull does take some eggs. Rockhopper parents are quite protective toward their young and react angrily whenever one of these predators hovers over their colonies in search of prey.

When they are approximately one month old it is time for the young rockhoppers to become more independent. It is also necessary for both parents to go to sea to find food. The chicks have grown rapidly and only one adult cannot bring sufficient nourishment each day.

During our studies we found that at one week old the young rockhoppers ate about 2 ounces of food a day. This amount rose gradually to over 20 ounces a day by the time they were taking maximum amounts of food from their parents.

Gradually the young start to wander a little distance from their nest sites, picking up an odd pebble or twig and engaging in what looks like making friends with neighboring birds. Groups of young rockhoppers, which may number only three or four or up to a dozen or more, then form *creches* or nursery groups. The downy rockhoppers remain close together during most of the day, while their parents make daily journeys to the sea to forage for food.

The rookery, therefore, breaks up into little groups of young and these are guarded or supervised by adults. From our observations of rockhoppers in the Falkland Islands, these "supervisors" are usually birds which have not bred successfully. When parent rockhoppers return from the sea they go straight to their nests and call. These calls immediately attract the young chicks, which break away from the creche to hurry to their nests to be fed. It is not uncommon for other young rockhoppers to wander round the colonies begging from different adult birds, but parents will only feed their own chicks.

Although the female birds seem to be responsible for most feeding in the early stages, male and female rockhoppers will feed the chicks as they grow older. Generally it seems that the female is the main feeder.

The creches or nursery groups are not always very close to some chicks' nest sites, but the particular voice of each parent bird is sufficient to trigger recognition in the young rockhopper penguin. By evening most of the creches break up as more and more parents return with food.

---

*Following: Guarded by small numbers of adults, the growing rockhopper chicks now form into nursery groups or creches.*

At approximately forty days old the chicks are about to shed their down. This is known as *molt*. The process is fairly rapid and starts to show on the tail and flippers, as well as around the face. Soon the dirty white breast down is replaced by bright new plumage and the fluffy overcoat gives way to sleek blue-black feathers on the back. The birds go through stages when they look immensely funny with patches of down clinging only to their backs, necks, or to the tops of their heads. Their behavior, too, can be most amusing at times, as they make strenuous efforts to

*The rockhopper chick, now near the end of its molt, still receives food from a parent. Soon it will be seeking its own at sea.*

*Rockhopper chick in new plumage. Wisps of down are all that remain of its first downy coat.*

flap their flippers at great speed, often hopping around and around on top of a flat rock while their winglike flippers beat the air. Their body size is still visibly smaller than that of their parents, but they have large feet and flippers.

Within two weeks or so the fully molted young rockhoppers enter the final stage in their short lives on the colony. They have not yet become acquainted with the feel of the sea. Their only experience with the ocean so far has been during stormy weather, when strong winds whip up the waves and clouds of spray lash the colonies.

While molting takes place, the parent birds continue their feeding trips, leaving the colonies in early morning to return in the

*In small groups, rock-hoppers come ashore at specially selected "landing places."*

afternoon or evening. In the particular colony we studied on New Island, the birds travel up and down the steep, narrow paths among the rocks and through tussock grass, jumping and hopping to and from the sea, seemingly never tiring. They are extremely surefooted and cling to sheer rock with their sharp toenails, sometimes aided by their powerful bills. Rockhoppers are some of the most resilient creatures we know. They have unbelievable strength and can survive enormous seas and violent weather.

Our rockhoppers come ashore onto a particular "landing place," a huge slab of rock which slopes into the sea at the bottom of three hundred-foot-high cliffs. On calm days the penguins can be seen far out at sea, their bodies silver in the sunlight as groups

make their porpoiselike movement toward the shore. With well-timed leaps from the surf, they deposit themselves on the rock without much effort, and then it is a long hop back up to the colony. When the seas are rough, and in these latitudes we can experience some terrific storms, the waves crash down against the rocks and threaten to smash any living creature. The tough little rockhoppers, however, come bravely ashore, getting thrown by the surf against the rocks, washed away and back again, sliding among the thick kelp seaweed beds before they reach safe rocky ground. Then they go on their way, often after no more than a brief pause to shake themselves and preen their feathers.

During some of these storms, when wind and driving rain and heavy seas pound the islands, those birds on the colonies are commonly seen lying squat on the ground facing away from the wind as if seeking shelter. Weather conditions such as these can affect young birds still in down, since their coats are not yet insulated like those of the adult birds. Mortality rates can be high if young are hit by cold and rain. We have seen as many as 30 percent of our "study" birds lost in the course of a day or two in such conditions.

When approaching the end of their molt, young rockhoppers are led by the adults to explore areas of the colony beyond their nest and creche sites. We have often seen an adult penguin hop-

*Thick beds of kelp seaweed may cover the approaches to the rockhopper landing places, making their landings even more formidable.*

ping from rock to rock with a trail of young birds following. Besides being something of an exploratory trip, this may also be a form of exercise for the chicks. A similar situation is often observed when parent birds come in to feed the already grown young. Rather than feed immediately, the adults encourage the young to follow them around parts of the rookery for several minutes before they stop to feed, often on top of a rock with the now large chicks below them.

Approximately in the middle of February time comes for the young rockhoppers to prepare to go to sea. They will follow those same routes down the rocky slopes which the older birds know so well. A number of newly molted birds were flipper-banded on New Island as part of our studies and to aid future identification. A wonderful sight met our eyes one day on a visit to the huge rock slabs at the base of the cliffs, below the rookery. Intermingled with large numbers of adult and subadult (one- to three-year-old) birds, we found increasing quantities of young penguins. These could be picked out by their slightly smaller and more slender size, the new plumage deeply tinged with blue, the dark bills, and absence of crests and the yellow trailing feathers. There could be no doubt that this was to be their first plunge into the sea, because their breasts were dirty and stained from the rookery.

Among this crowd of thousands we were delighted to spot one of our first banded young! (The chick had been banded that same season up on the colony and was now found at the bottom of the cliffs near the landing zone.) This, with some ten others and some older birds, was watched for quite some time. There is a particular area of rocky shore used by these penguins as their departure point. From there they plunge into the sea—sometimes in a neat dive but on most occasions they just plummet feet first! These newcomers to the sea now wandered warily back and forth along the rocky shoreline, peering occasionally into the deep rumbling water below. Now and again an adult bird would take the plunge, surface, and then call, and several young ones bravely would follow. Our banded rockhopper chicks had gone to sea for the first time. It was clear from watching the penguin chicks that they were quite inexperienced. On hitting the water they tended to flounder and thrash the surface with their flippers, but once underwater they showed superb coordination and they moved quickly and without hesitation. These young rockhoppers were then slightly over two months old. Within ten days or so not one young bird could be found on the colony. A new period of their lives would now begin at sea.

The Magellan penguin chicks live an early life of seclusion. They do not come out from the depths of their burrows until they are about three-quarters grown. Parent birds bring food to the downy chicks, giving them this food in the same manner as do the rockhoppers. The Magellan's food is usually composed of small schooling fishes.

In the Falkland Islands, the young Magellan penguins do not form creches or nursery groups, but in January the chicks start to

*Young Magellan penguin at the entrance to its burrow among tussock grass.*

*An adult Magellan with its newly molted youngster.*

appear outside the nests. However, they do not venture farther
than the entrances to the burrows, and are rarely left uncared for
by the parents.

Molt in the young Magellans starts by the end of January. As
in the case of the rockhoppers, the process can be over in about
ten days. Soon these birds, too, will begin a cycle of their lives
at sea. Their first trip down to the water is not as hazardous as that
of the rockhoppers, since their burrows are generally near beaches

*Immature Magellan penguin about to shed its coat after many months at sea.*

or sandy shores. Their first plunge therefore is made in tame, shallow waters, but they can be seen warily testing the sea, splashing along the shoreline, then returning to the safety of the beach.

The early life of a gentoo penguin resembles that of a rockhopper chick. Through the rearing states, it stays in the colonies and receives food and protection from the parent birds. The young

*Gentoo feeding chick by regurgitation.*

*Young gentoo begging for food from its parent.*

gentoos experience quite a rapid rate of growth and soon are the size of the adults. These very fat, down-covered birds are most amusing to watch, and they appear to enjoy watching humans! If you sit quietly a little distance from the colony, it is not unusual for small groups of young gentoos to come gingerly right up and peer curiously at you. However, a noise or cumbersome movement on your part will send the young birds hurrying back to the colony. Usually curiosity gets the better of them, and soon they return to view the intruder once more.

*Gentoo chick seeking shelter beneath its parent.*

Gentoos often rear two chicks which, after completing their molt, gather into groups near coasts and beaches. In the same way as we have seen in the rockhopper colonies, the young birds appear to be enticed, or led, by adult birds to the beaches. In the case of the gentoo young this may take some days, for although the route to the landing beach may not be so formidable, the distance can be considerable. We know of some colonies which are over three miles from the landing beach, and the young birds seem to take the trip in stages. Like the Magellan penguin young, the gentoos take to the sea in a gradual manner, at first splashing in and out of the shallows, later taking to the water fully, diving

*Immature gentoos come to peer at the photographer.*

and swimming a short distance. But even in these early attempts they show instinctive ease and agility, their streamlined shapes darting below the surface most gracefully.

These young gentoos and their older companions do not leave the neighborhood of the Falkland Islands in the wintertime. They move from the breeding colonies to beaches where they can rest. This movement away from the breeding grounds is very important because it allows the winter winds, rain, and snow effectively to clean the colonies before another breeding cycle begins the following spring.

# 4
# The King Penguin

Although king penguins (*Aptenodytes patagonica*) are found in large numbers on other islands farther south, there are only small numbers of them breeding in the Falkland Islands. Here they are found normally in the vicinity or company of gentoos. Their pattern of breeding is quite different from other penguins and a visit to a king penguin colony during the summer presents a rather confusing picture. There may be adult birds with eggs or chicks, birds with grown young, birds in molt, and immature birds.

The king penguin's breeding cycle usually takes fourteen months to complete. Rockhoppers, gentoos, Magellans, and macaroni take only five months. This means that kings are able to rear only one chick two seasons in three. The earliest period of courtship and mating of the kings in the Falklands is during early November, eggs being laid about mid-November. Like the emperor penguin of Antarctica—the only other species of penguin which has a similar and extended breeding period—the king lays only one

*Small breeding colony of king penguins. These birds are incubating the single egg, which is held on top of their feet and enveloped by a fold of skin.*

egg, and does not build a nest. Instead, the egg is held on the upper surface of the bird's feet and then enveloped in a fold of loose body skin.

Incubation of the rather large egg (mean diameter about 3 inches) continues for some fifty-four days, during which time both female and male birds share incubation. While the egg is held on the top of the feet, the bird sits back on its thick padded heels, with toes raised off the ground. In this way the egg tends to rest back against the body. When changing over incubation, the king penguins first call and display to each other. The partner holding the egg then straightens up from its crouched incubating position, lowers the toes, and allows the egg to roll onto the ground. Immediately its mate hooks its bill over the egg and draws it onto its own feet, finally adopting the incubation position itself.

After hatching, the young chick is reared by both parents in the same manner as we have described in the other species. However, in the early stages a chick may be brooded or cared for by other parents. Some five to six weeks after hatching, the young kings gather into nursery groups, but break away to join their

*Creche of young kings, dressed in their thick down. Photographed in winter, the chicks are about two-thirds of the way through the twelve to fourteen month rearing period.*

parents when these return with food. Like the rockhopper chicks, the kings learn to recognize the calls of the returning parents. This is called by biologists *imprinting,* and is the recognition of a parent's call by the young bird—in much the same way that a young child quickly learns to recognize the sound of its parents' voices. Just how important these calls are, I was to discover when recording the calls of the adult birds.

Having made my recordings, I sat some distance away from the colony to play back the tape. Being a very quiet evening, the recording was heard by a small group of chicks nearby, which answered with their piping calls. They quickly left the creche to come to where I was sitting, convinced no doubt that I could fulfill their needs of food!

For some ten months or more the young king penguins are fed by the parents, and they grow rapidly to enormous proportions in the early stages. Growth slows down through the midwinter period and then progresses again in the spring. At this time the chick starts to molt its down for a coat similar to that of an adult's plumage but far less colorful. Like many birds, all penguins take one or two years before they attain the generally more colorful plumage of adults. Some three to four weeks after this molt starts, the young bird leaves the colony on its first journey to the sea. Over eleven months may now have passed since the chick emerged from the egg.

After this long rearing stage, the parent kings take a rest by feeding at sea for a period of two to three weeks, where they gain

*Pair of adult king penguins in the midst of a colony of gentoo. Note the kings' very large feet and heels.*

weight to return to shore and go through their own molt. After this stage they go to sea again, for another two to three weeks, to feed and regain lost weight. By the time they return to the breeding grounds to commence another breeding cycle, some fourteen months or more have passed since the start of the previous cycle. So it is that the pair we have seen laying their egg the previous November, now lay their new egg perhaps in January. However, by the time they have completed this second breeding cycle— taking perhaps another fourteen months—their third cycle cannot commence before the month of March. March is the beginning of fall and very late for birds to start to breed. Therefore this pair of king penguins will not breed in this third season. Thus we see how they only produce two chicks in three years. In the following season—fourth year—the pair returns to the colony early, and so the whole process starts again. Realizing that all pairs of king penguins do not follow the same pattern as each other, it is possible to understand why so many different "stages" can be seen on a colony during the summer period.

*Immature rockhopper penguin, known as a "graybeard." After molt, the bird will take on the appearance of an adult.*

# 5

# The Family Group
# and Molting

Toward the end of the first week in December, when the first rockhopper chicks start to emerge from the eggs, numbers of plump-looking rockhoppers start to appear in the rookeries. Although dressed in adult plumage, they contrast with the adult parents which return to feed the newly hatched chicks. While the parents go about the colonies in a determined manner, intent on reaching their partners and in so doing making extensive greeting calls, these other arrivals stand about the edges of the rookeries, apparently interested only in looking over the "family" gatherings. From our studies on New Island we have learned that many of these are birds that have lost their mates earlier in the season. The urge, or instinct, to return to the rookery, however, is as great as that of their companions that are fortunate to have a mate and now a chick to rear.

Although these single birds do not appear to have any position in the colonies at such times, we have speculated that they play a useful part. At the same time these birds make an appearance, there also arrive small groups of immature rockhoppers. These were often named *graybeards* by early sealers and penguin-oilers. This name is very fitting, for, instead of the distinct black-and-white pattern on the throat of the older birds, these younger penguins have an indistinct line which gives the appearance of a gray beard. Like their older companions, these younger birds are plump with accumulations of fat. This is their first time back on the colony since they left as chicks the year before, having spent the time in between living at sea. Besides the indistinct throat pattern, these younger arrivals lack the defined crest of the adults. When they first left the rookeries they had black bills; now they wear the reddish-brown colored bills of adult birds.

There are many unanswered questions about these younger penguins. For example, where are they when the adult birds first return to the colonies in the spring? There is no indication that they swim back to the Islands with the adult birds when these return from migration, waiting several weeks to come ashore. Yet we guess these younger birds must follow the same migratory routes. What may happen is that the young penguins stay with the unattached adults, and that together they complete the return journey to the rookery of their birth, where they will molt.

Living for much of their lives in a watery environment, penguins need the protection of their fat and also their rather stiff, oily-tipped feathers. Unable to shed their feathers at sea, they must come ashore to do this. Unlike most other birds, molting is quite rapid in penguins, all feathers being changed within two weeks. During the period of molt the penguins cannot enter the sea to feed. They lose a lot of their insulation as the old feathers are shed. So as to prepare for this period ashore with no food, and perhaps bitter weather, they arrive on the colonies with a store of rations in the form of a thick layer of fat beneath the skin. In our studies of rockhoppers we weighed many birds as they came ashore at this time, and found that male adult birds—normally heavier than the female—weighed some ten pounds. By the time they had completed their molt and were ready to return to the sea, they had lost half of this weight. A similar weight loss was found in the female birds.

Generally those penguins returning to the colonies to molt in December are composed of one class of younger birds, one-year-old birds or graybeards, excepting of course the few older, single birds of which we have spoken before. After these birds have completed their molt they return to the sea. However, there are other classes or "age groups" yet to arrive in the colonies and molt. In fact there will be three different periods when groups of penguins are ashore to molt. We have seen one group molt and leave for the sea again. By the first week in February another age group is ashore and molting. These are generally what we may call nonbreeding birds, penguins perhaps two to three years old that have yet to start breeding.

The feathers of these birds arriving to molt in February are often

*Immature rockhoppers return to the colonies of their birth to molt. Note the lack of a full crest on the younger bird (center) with two adults.*

the same as adults' but appear rather dull, with a brownish coloring. After a few days ashore the appearance of these birds changes dramatically. They stand almost lifeless, apparently completely disinterested in all about them. Instead of a streamlined look to their plumage, this now starts to fluff out as though they were wearing coats too large for them. Some days later the coats com-

*During their molt, rockhoppers appear to be wearing coats too large for them. This is due to the old feathers remaining attached to the tips of the new ones.*

mence to molt from about their tails. Beneath can be seen the bright steely-blue of new feathers. Gradually the molt progresses, and the birds become more active, preening out the old feathers.

At the height of the molt, when the winds cut across the colonies, one might liken the scene to that of a snowstorm but with feathers swirling about instead of snowflakes. During the latter part of the molt penguins look even more comical, with remnants of old feathering forming "scarves" about their necks or "hats" which contrast with the new plumage. As the old feathers molt away they sometimes remain partially attached to the tips of the new feathers, until finally breaking away. At this stage penguins look twice their normal size, and their crests seem to develop enormous proportions due to the old feathers remaining attached to the tips of new ones.

Returning briefly to look at the gentoo chicks, we have mentioned that they too are in full molt.

In the gentoo colonies, the chicks have now grown to a stage where they start to molt their down. As in the older birds, molt starts about the tail. The stiff tail feathers appear for the first time. The flippers then lose their down, as do areas about the eyes. Final molt takes place about the back of the head. Now the young chicks take on a completely new look, their plumage having a lovely blue

*At the height of molt, feathers drift over the penguin colonies like snow, and many birds take on a ridiculous appearance.*

*Young gentoos about three-quarters grown. The center bird has yet to receive its daily feed—note the contrast with the extended stomachs of its companions.*

tinge and just the faintest sign of what will be a white mark on the head.

As molt progresses in the gentoo chicks, they become more active, moving about the immediate area of the rookeries and rapidly exercising their flippers as though attempting to fly. Even at this stage of growth the adults return to feed the chicks. Activity increases as returning parents are chased around the colonies by their offspring clamoring for food. This helps the young birds develop their feet and legs and builds up their muscles in preparation for the day when they must leave the colonies.

This chasing is one of the most amusing scenes which takes place in the gentoo penguin colonies. In such colonies the "chase" by chicks can be prolonged, with sometimes two or even three young birds chasing an adult around and around or through a colony for several minutes. The adult always maintains the lead, with the gasping and rather fat chick (or chicks) trailing a very small distance behind, often tripping over its own feet. Eventually, when it looks like the chick is about exhausted, the adult bird halts and feeds the young penguin.


Returning to the rockhopper rookery, we have seen one group of birds arrive, molt, and leave. A second age group is now completing its molt and moving closer to the water's edge in preparation for leaving. It is now mid-February and late summer. At this point, the young rockhoppers are fully molted and they too move away from their nest and creche sites.

In the same colony, yet another important part of the penguin's life has been taking place. Among the many birds which come ashore to molt during early February, there are a number of birds which have not reached the age when they will breed successfully, but they are preparing for this event. Although too late in the

*King cormorants nest among the rockhoppers.*

season to commence breeding, these penguins start courtship and display to each other frequently. They select sites and build nests and may even attempt mating. Their activities finally stop and they begin to molt. In the following season, these birds will probably join older breeding pairs to attempt their first breeding season.

As the rockhopper chicks leave, so the rookeries clear of adult birds also taking to the sea. Parents have spent over two months going back and forth between land and sea fetching food for their offspring. Many of these adults are visibly thin, and now it is time to spend a period at sea to feed and gain back that weight. In our observations of young leaving, we have seen adults encouraging them to follow into the water. We have often heard those birds calling as they swam off, so it would be reasonable to believe that chick and parent probably keep company for a time at sea. But not for long, for by mid-March those parent birds now return to their nest sites. Coming back now to molt, they have prepared themselves for their enforced stay ashore and they are fat and heavy. Their feathers are dull and worn. So it is that the third and last group of rockhoppers starts to molt.

We believe from our studies that pairs of birds probably remain together at sea. Certainly they are capable of finding each other, for although partners were known to leave at different periods on this feeding trip before their molt, many pairs returned to the colony together. Those birds which did not join up earlier, met at their nest sites with a great deal of display.

With this molt of the adult rockhoppers, another breeding season comes to a close. The rookery is again packed with birds, but there is a different feeling to the scene. It is almost a tired feeling, a feeling that the birds themselves are anxious to lose their old feathers and be away again. Fall is approaching and it is time for the rockhoppers to migrate.

The king cormorants, which share the colonies, have already seen their young fly and have themselves left. Only the young black-browed albatrosses sit patiently until they lose all their down and can also fly. By the end of the first week in April, the rockhoppers have almost completed their molt. By the third week all the birds will have gone from the large New Island rookery.

# 6

# Penguins at Sea

Gradually we are learning more about the life of penguins at sea, but still most of what we do know is restricted to feeding and enemies of penguins at sea. Little is known of their swimming, diving, and migration. On New Island we have attempted to follow penguins at sea, hopefully to learn a little more about these birds in the environment to which they are best adapted. The task is difficult indeed and only shows more clearly just how penguins master their watery world.

To swim, the birds propel themselves with their flippers and use downward thrusts, the tail acting rather like the rudder of a ship. The tail feathers of penguins are generally stiff, forming what we may describe as a *keel* shape—not only in the collective form but each individual feather. This, no doubt, plays an important part in their swimming abilities. Some penguins, like the king, make use of the tail on land as a "prop," as they lean back on the soles of their feet while resting or incubating.

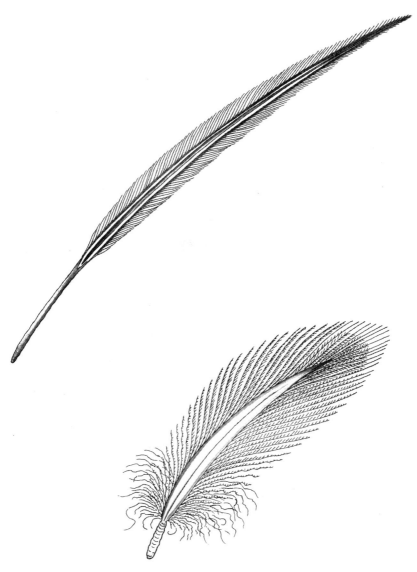

*Tail feather of gentoo penguin. View underneath showing "hollow keel" of the feather's shaft. Below: A much enlarged drawing of a body feather with its broad stiff shaft and fine filaments at the base which give extra insulation by holding air.*

98

*Note the size of these rockhopper chicks' feet. They are almost as large as the adults'.*

Although the feet of penguins are webbed, they do not appear to be used while swimming and diving. While on the surface of the sea or bathing in shallow rock pools, the feet and webs are used but still appear to be secondary to their flippers. We mentioned earlier the large size of the young rockhoppers' feet and

99

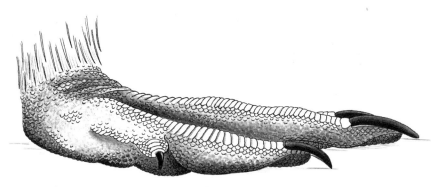

*Detail of gentoo penguin foot showing the typical tough leather-like form of penguin feet.*

flippers. Measurements taken just before they left for the sea for the first time showed that these were almost adult size, yet their bodies were much smaller. This is obviously one of nature's compensations, enabling the young birds to keep up the same swimming ability as the adults during their early lives at sea.

While traveling at sea many penguin species seem to *porpoise*, swimming a short distance underwater, then making a leap above the surface. This is commonly seen in gentoos and rockhoppers. We have only observed Magellans doing this when they were being chased by seals.

From the type of food taken by most of the Falkland species of penguins, the birds do not need to dive to any great depths and probably they remain within a few feet of the surface. Recent studies of the larger penguins such as the king, however, have shown that penguins can dive to depths of six hundred feet in search of food. Rockhoppers can remain underwater for a minute or more, while the larger species may remain below for at least three minutes. To compensate their breathing, they rely on amounts of dissolved oxygen in their blood, while the heart rate drops to as much as one-twentieth of the normal rate.

We have described the feathers of penguins and how they give insulation properties to the body. Remaining as they do for many weeks at sea, the feathers must also waterproof the body. The oily tips effectively repel the seawater and give a smooth streamlining to the body. But beneath the tips, the lower sections of the shafts of the feathers support soft, downy filaments, which in effect create an "undercoat" which traps quantities of air. This adds insulation and acts as additional waterproofing.

While watching rockhoppers in their colonies, we noticed they drank large amounts of fresh water. Penguins need fresh water to keep their blood and other body fluids at the correct concentrations. Some supply of fresh water in the colonies is so important that this would probably have been paramount when the penguins first selected their breeding places many thousands of years ago. How is it, then, that they can cope with seawater?

At sea they distill their fresh-water requirements by using special glands situated in their nasal tubes. These glands remove the salts from the seawater, and the salts are then discharged through the nostrils on the tops of their bills. It is not uncommon to see groups of rockhoppers, shortly after arrival from the sea, apparently suffering from "runny noses" until these salts are discharged.

As mentioned, most species of penguin are believed to take

their food from close to the sea's surface, except perhaps the deep divers, the king and emperor penguins. Perhaps the most important food of those penguins which live in the southern oceans is *krill*. Krill is a collective name given to several species of shrimp-like crustaceans. In Antarctic waters probably the most important of these is one called *Euphausia superba*. Farther north, in the waters about the Falklands, we are more familiar with lobster krill (*Munida gregaria*). Both these types of krill form shoals so large and dense that hundreds of square yards of ocean sometimes appear red from the color of these creatures. Even flying one or two thousand feet above the sea on our way to or from New Island at certain periods of the summer, one can see these shoals spread out into long, pink streams, as currents and tides carry them along.

Other important foods are squid and small schooling fishes. In the case of those penguins found off South Africa, Chile, Peru, and Argentina, these form the main food supply. We believe from our studies on rockhoppers that this species is probably selective in its feeding. For example, during the early stages of chick growth, the adults bring quantities of very small krill on which to feed the young birds. Later, when the chicks are more than half grown, the diet changes to squid and small fish. Gentoo penguins feed largely on lobster krill, while Magellan penguins appear to favor small schooling fishes.

Penguins have specially adapted tongues and mouths lined with small fleshy spines, which point back toward the throat. These help to hold prey while water is filtered off.

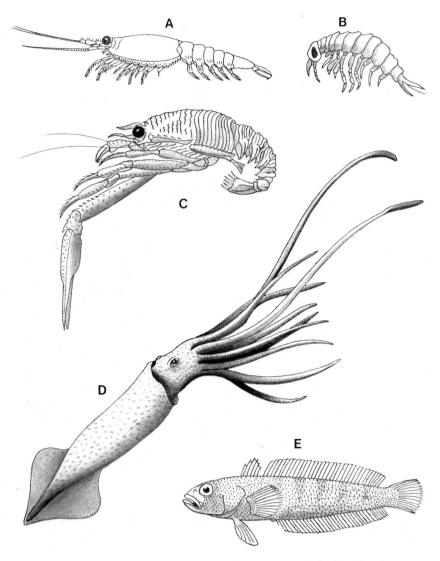

*Some different forms of penguin food. A. Type of krill—Euphausian species. B. Species of Amphipod. C. Lobster krill, an important food of Falkland species of penguin. D. Squid, an important feed of all forms of penguins. E. Notothenid fish, another important food of some species of penguins.*

103

One matter on which we still must guess is exactly how penguins seek their food. We assume that sight is used in most cases, but do they also detect large shoals of krill, fish, and squid by sound? Using a sensitive underwater microphone we have listened to the amazing variety of sounds produced by marine life. It is known that whales, dolphins, and porpoises are capable of detecting shoals of krill by the sounds these creatures make. It is possible that penguins can detect their prey in the same manner.

MIGRATION

Not all penguins migrate from their breeding areas. In the Falklands there is evidence to show that gentoo and king penguins move only short distances away from the islands. The yellow-eyed penguin of southern New Zealand is one species which keeps very close to its breeding grounds all year round. The rockhopper, macaroni, and Magellan penguins on the Falklands, on the other hand, make considerable journeys away from the breeding grounds during the winter period.

So as to understand something of these migrations, first we shall look at the seas about the Falklands, in particular the movement of the seas or currents. These are caused by three main forces: prevailing winds; differences in the sea's density or salinity, amounts of salts in the water; and the earth's rotation. Where currents meet or diverge, where cold or salty water sinks due to a meeting with a less dense water, or where coast winds blow the

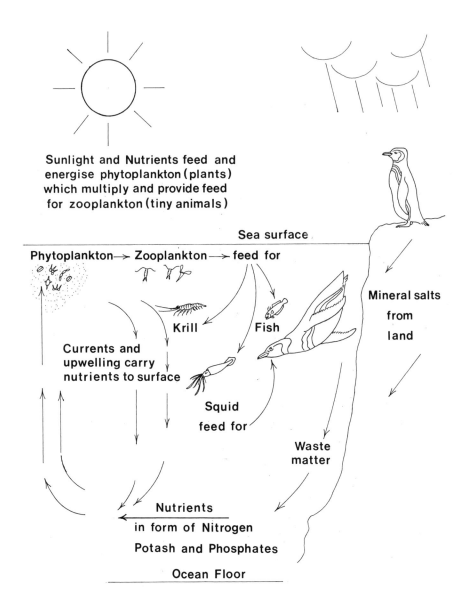

Sunlight and Nutrients feed and
energise phytoplankton (plants)
which multiply and provide feed
for zooplankton (tiny animals)

Sea surface

Phytoplankton → Zooplankton → feed for

Krill

Fish

Mineral salts
from
land

Currents and
upwelling carry
nutrients to surface

Squid
feed for

Waste
matter

Nutrients
in form of Nitrogen
Potash and Phosphates

Ocean Floor

*Diagram showing food chain or cycle of the Southern Oceans involving the penguin species.*

surface of the water seaward, a movement is set up which may touch the ocean bottom.

The surface waters are then replaced by upwelling of waters rich in nutrients from the ocean floor. These in turn stimulate the new growth of marine plants—known as phytoplankton—on which microscopic animal life feeds. These microscopic creatures are known as zooplankton (from the Greek meaning "animals that drift") and include krill. Zooplankton are preyed upon by larger animals, which in turn provide food for even larger creatures, and so a cycle commences.

Perhaps one of the greatest and richest currents in terms of food is one which circles the Southern Ocean and is known as the West Wind Drift. As this current moves from west to east it passes the tip of South America and Cape Horn, there picking up richer waters off the Antarctic continent. As an offshoot of this larger current, a smaller current known as the Falkland Current, sweeps up toward the Falkland Islands. It passes each side and continues northward up the coast of Argentina.

There is still much to be learned of this current, but what is evident is that at certain times of the year it is rich in forms of zooplankton, including krill. With its steady flow past the Falklands, there is a continuous supply of food available for the penguins and other animal life.

At certain times of the year, coinciding with the main breeding period of the penguins and other seabirds, the amount of food carried by this current increases. During the latter part of the

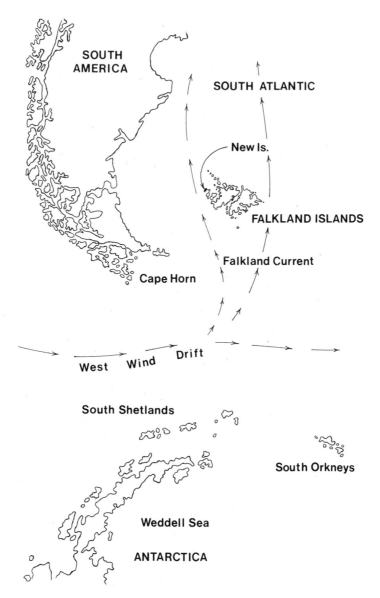

*Map showing position of Falkland Islands in relation to South America and Antarctica, and direction of the West Wind Drift and the Falkland Current.*

summer, when the young penguins require large amounts of food, the amounts of krill about these waters increases. However, as the current continues to flow north, so must a certain amount of the food be carried northward. It is just after this influx of food starts to diminish about the Falklands' waters, that we notice the penguins leaving with other seabirds.

We know from observations that the birds move northward so that, being dependent on certain food moved by the current, a migration develops to follow this food. The Falkland Current travels only so far north before it disperses at a point just off the mouth of the River Plate (some 1,200 miles north of the Falklands between Buenos Aires, Argentina, and Uruguay). At this point, too, we believe the travels of our penguins also halt before they start their journey back to the Falklands so as to arrive in time to start another breeding season. Undoubtedly other forces play a part in the movement of these birds. The story is far from complete, but perhaps the birds should keep some of their secrets.

## PREDATION

One of the most amazing sights we have watched many times is the arrival of thousands of rockhoppers at their landing places during storms. Even so, of the vast numbers of penguins which take part in these landings during a breeding season, we have yet to find a bird which had been killed by such a situation. During continuous bad weather and heavy seas, when a parent bird returns each day to the rookery to bring food, we have noted that birds get

*Giant petrel on its nest. These birds frequent landing places, taking weak or injured penguins from the sea.*

visibly tired. In extreme cases it is possible that returning birds may become prey to groups of giant petrels, large seabirds which lie in wait offshore for weakened birds.

*Adult male—bull—sea lions have developed a habit in some areas of preying on penguins.*

On New Island and many other places in the Falklands where such landing places exist for rockhoppers and other penguins, it is not unusual to find sea lions living in the vicinity. Our own observations have found that these are usually old male animals, apparently living a life on their own, perhaps outcasts from their own herds. These animals prey on the penguins as they are about to land. They may even give chase to groups of birds as they scramble up the rocky shores, seizing one unlucky individual, which will be taken back into the sea. The curious thing is that although these penguins will be eaten at times by a sea lion, very often they are tossed and thrashed about on the water's surface by the seal, only to be left for the giant petrels.

The penguin is not a natural prey for these seals, which normally feed on octopus, squid, and fish. Why they should take penguins is yet to be explained.

In southern waters the leopard seal is a predator of penguins, taking birds as food. The proportion in relation to this seal's other food is not known, so we can only guess at the effect this may have on total populations of penguins. However, biologists working on colonies of Antarctic penguins report that, in some cases, leopard seals live in the vicinity of penguin rookeries throughout the breeding periods, apparently living entirely off penguins.

Killer whales are reputed to take a heavy toll of penguins at sea, but there is no substantial evidence of this. We can only guess. Penguins would be small prey for such a large creature but as these predators work in groups, it is possible that large numbers

*Killer whale chasing penguins.*

of penguins at sea may be "herded" and taken in numbers by the killer whales.

We have noted that penguins are able to identify a predator. For example, a number of fur seals playing on one of the rockhopper landing areas did not appear to cause too much alarm to landing birds; neither does the appearance of elephant seals. But the appearance of a sea lion causes the reverse!

In a similar way, the presence of a pod of killer whales just

*Rockhopper penguins show no fear of certain species of seal, such as this immature sea elephant.*

*Adélie penguins undisturbed by the presence of an elephant seal on*

*their rookery.*

offshore from a landing beach used by gentoo penguins caused great panic among the birds. This is the only evidence known to us personally that those animals probably do take penguins at sea.

Sadly, the most substantial evidence we have of a form of predation at sea is one caused directly by man himself. Every year we find increasing numbers of "oiled" penguins, slowly dying from the effects of being covered by thick deposits of oil. The birds we find ashore must be a small percentage of the total numbers which die at sea as the result of this menace. Where this oil originally comes from we do not know, but its presence fits the increase of fishing fleets now appearing in the southern seas, and the intensified search for oil off the Patagonian coast.

# 7

# Man and Penguins

The natives of southern South America, South Africa, and New Zealand knew and must have used penguins as important sources of meat, oil, and skins. Before 1499, however, the birds were probably unknown to peoples living in the Northern Hemisphere. It was in 1499, when the voyage of Vasco da Gama was made to India, that a description was written of birds off the South African coast "as large as ganders and with a cry resembling the braying of asses, which could not fly." This is almost certainly what we know today as the jackass (or black-footed) penguin.

In 1519, Magellan made his epic trip south and discovered the Straits—now called Magellan—between Tierra del Fuego and the coast of Patagonia. A scholar on board Magellan's ship *Trinidad* wrote of large flocks of "strange geese" which were recorded by him as "penguins." This seems to be the first time the name was given to the birds, and most likely it came from the Latin *pinguis*, meaning fat.

*During late summer, the Magellans group together to molt.*

When Sir Francis Drake sailed from England on his famous circumnavigation in 1577, he knew of the existence of penguins and when he sailed into the Straits of Magellan in August, 1578, he described the birds on "Penguin Island." From his mention of penguins living in burrows, we judge he referred to what we know today as the Magellan penguin. This is an interesting point, for today these birds only return to their breeding grounds early in September. Drake took quantities of these birds to restock his ship, as did a succession of other voyagers.

In 1592, John Davis, an English navigator, with his ship *Desire* was also in the area of the Straits of Magellan when a storm drove him east to the Falkland Islands, and thus they were discovered. Davis did not land, so we don't know whether he was aware of the large populations of penguins on these islands. He too visited Drake's "Penguin Island" to stock his vessel.

A few years later Sir Richard Hawkins visited "Penguin Island" and wrote of the likeness of penguin meat with that of puffins, with which he was familiar from the islands off the south coast of England. Hawkins salted down many barrels of penguins, and records of other mariners mention as many as fifty thousand birds being taken by single expeditions.

In 1758 Linnaeus gave the first scientific description and name to a penguin; this was the South African "jackass" penguin. Some sixteen other species were then to be named over the next century or so. The first specimens of emperor penguins, although probably seen by earlier voyagers, were not identified and collected until 1839-43, during the Ross Expedition to Antarctica. The first colony of emperors was not found until Scott's Expedition in 1901-04.

In the year 1764, Louis de Bougainville led an expedition to the Falkland Islands for the purpose of settlement. In one of his narratives he describes a king penguin which was kept and tamed.

This appears to be the first description written of any species of penguin in these Islands.

A few years later, the commander of a British settlement at the Falklands, Lt. Samuel Clayton, described four kinds: "the yellow or king penguin, the red, the black or holey—from their burrowing underground—and the jumping jacks, from their motion." (The "red" would have been the gentoo, "black or holey" the Magellan, and "jumping jack" the rockhopper.) Clayton mentions the eggs being "good nourishing food" but considered the flesh unfit to eat. This opinion of the penguins' flesh was later taken up by many other voyagers, for some years later we find little mention of the birds being used for food. Their eggs continued to be prized for many more years to come.

With the discovery of the Falkland Islands and their vast wealth of seals, whales, and penguins, expeditions soon began to set out from Europe and the United States to take oils and skins. At first these voyagers were content to take those animals which yielded the greatest return for the labor, that is, seals and whales. Penguin eggs, however, continued to be a valuable source of food.

Toward the latter part of the 1700s, New Island itself was a favorite overwintering place for American whalers and sealers. They wrote of the rockhopper rookery where many of our studies are made today, as the site of their egg collecting, and told how many thousands of eggs were stored each season. These were preserved by immersing them in seal oil and then stored in barrels through the winter.

Eventually, seals and whales alone were not to satisfy the oiling expeditions and some time in the 1820s, penguins were being taken and put into the try-pots to be boiled out for their oil.

Few records exist to give us an idea of how extensive this industry was in the Falklands. We do know, however, from records that between 1864 and 1866 certain islands in the Falklands were cleared of penguins by the oilers, producing some sixty-three thousand gallons of oil. These exploitations probably resulted in the death of over half a million penguins.

From the evidence remaining to this day, in the form of rough stone-walled corrals where the penguins were herded for killing,

*Author's wife stands in the center of a penguin corral on New Island, indicating the entrance through which the penguins would have been herded.*

it is possible that many more birds were taken, for in those days there was little control of this business and limited interest in keeping records. The business did not take place only in the Falklands. At South Georgia, vast numbers of birds were taken each year. Probably the most famous penguin oiling operation was that on Macquarie Island, where the business started in 1891 and continued for more than twenty-five years, taking royal penguins. A public outcry finally stopped the trade.

The taking of penguin eggs in the Falkland Islands was to

*The author on the perimeter of a very large mixed colony of rockhopper penguins and black-browed albatrosses. He estimated this colony contained over two million birds.*

become almost a tradition with settlers, and not so many years ago, a date—usually about November 9—was fixed for the start of Egging Week. For people living in the capital town of Stanley, the season was marked by the arrival of local cutter boats, bringing in many thousands of eggs which were sold on the public jetty. Today, egging continues under license but it is a tradition which is dying out.

In more recent years, the Falkland Islands have had better communications with the outside world. This has brought in many

*Author's daughter making friends with king cormorants and rock-hoppers.*

visitors interested in seeing the large colonies of penguins and other wildlife. We believe this has introduced to the Islands a new awareness of our wildlife and the need to conserve it. Many islands occupied by large colonies of penguins have now been set aside as reserves, with laws to protect the birds.

In Antarctica, the home of large populations of penguins, the

Antarctic Treaty, an agreement signed by many nations to acknowledge this vast area as a form of international reserve, the penguins and other natural life are effectively conserved. However, we believe that man himself poses a new threat to the lives of penguins, especially those species which live in these regions. We have pointed out the importance of krill, squid, and schooling fishes as food for the penguins. Less than ten years ago, competition for this food was among the whales, seals, and seabirds alone. Today man, in his ever-increasing search for new sources of food, has started to reap the southern seas. Fleets of trawlers and factory ships ply these oceans, in their search for shoals of krill, fish, and squid. It has been said that the southern oceans can yield millions of tons annually without endangering the supply to other life which relies directly on this food, but do we know? The same was said about whales many years ago, yet we now are desperately attempting to save some species of whales from extinction.

So often we exploit nature until it is too late. We can only hope that nations may look back at their mistakes and ensure for the sake of our penguins that we do not do the same.

# Index